THIS BOOK
BELONGS TO

BUSINESS BASICS FOR KIDS

LEARN WITH LEMONADE STAND

PROFIT AND LOSS

DAY 1:SUNNY DAY

ANDRE SETS UP HIS LEMONADE STAND ON A NICE WARM AND SUNNY DAY.

EVERY DAY ANDRE GOES TO THE STORE AND BUYS INGREDIENTS NEEDED TO PREPARE HIS LEMONADE.

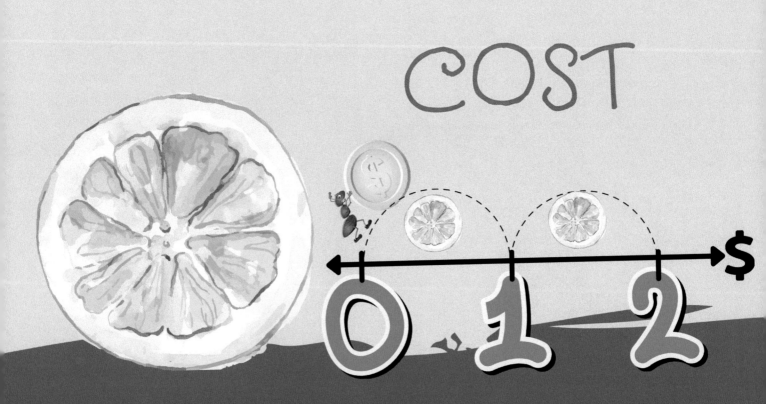

HE BUYS TWO
LEMONS FOR $2.

Two Dollars

HE BUYS ONE CUP OF SUGAR FOR $1.

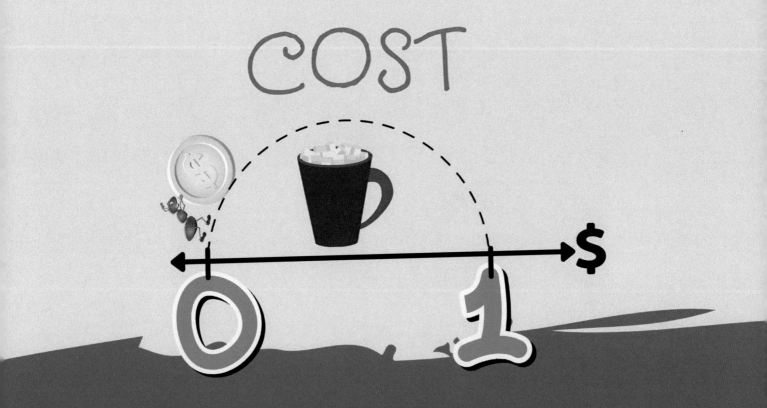

One Dollar

Sunny Day Cost

TWO LEMONS

1 CUP SUGAR

Total Cost

$2

+

$1

$3

ANDRE PREPARES FOUR GLASSES OF LEMONADE EVERY DAY IN THE MORNING USING TWO LEMONS AND ONE CUP OF SUGAR

Sunny Day Sales

ANDRE SELLS **FOUR GLASSES** OF LEMONADE AT THE END OF DAY 1 FOR **$1** EACH.

Total Sales

Four Dollars

Sunny Day Profit

 SALES   **—** $4

TOTAL COST $3

  +

Profit $1

ANDRE MADE A NICE PROFIT OF $1 AT END OF DAY 1. *Yippie!!!*

RAIN STARTS TO
POUR ON THE
SECOND DAY.

Rainy Day Cost

TWO LEMONS

1 CUP SUGAR

Total Cost

$2

$+$

$1

$3

ANDRE HAS THE SAME TOTAL COST FOR RAINY AND SUNNY DAYS BECAUSE HE PREPARES HIS LEMONADE AT THE START OF EACH DAY.

Rainy Day Sales

ANDRE SELLS **TWO GLASSES** OF LEMONADE AT THE END OF DAY 2 FOR **$1** EACH.

Total Sales

Two Dollars

Rainy Day Loss

 SALES   — $2

TOTAL COST $3

  +

LOSS   ($1)

ANDRE MADE A LOSS
OF $1 AT END OF
DAY 2.

Ouch!

PROFIT

AMOUNT OF MONEY THAT YOU GET TO KEEP AFTER PAYING FOR ALL COSTS IS CALLED PROFIT.

PROFIT IS ALWAYS A "POSITIVE" NUMBER.
EXAMPLE: :+$100

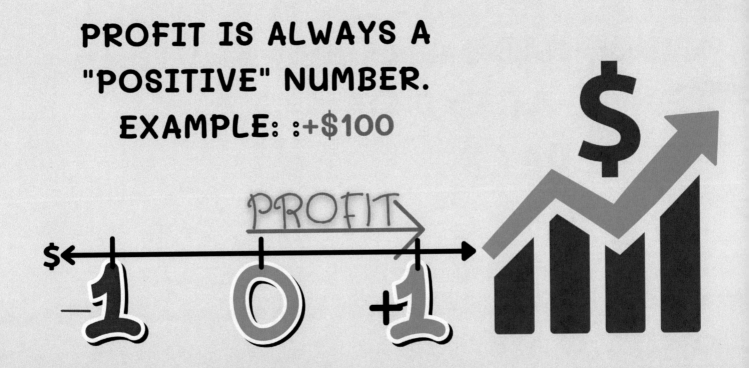

PROFIT

$ -1   0   +1

LOSS

THE AMOUNT OF MONEY THAT YOU STILL NEED TO PAY AFTER ACCOUNTING FOR ALL PROFITS IS CALLED LOSS.

LOSS IS ALWAYS A "NEGATIVE" NUMBER.
EXAMPLE: :-$100

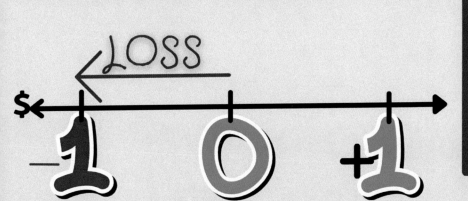

LOSS.

TO MAKE MORE PROFITS REDUCE YOUR COSTS. INCREASE YOUR SALES.

EXPAND YOUR BUSINESS BY BUILDING MORE LEMONADE STANDS

Made in the USA
Middletown, DE
30 October 2023

41673792R00018